Sp

Aa
Bb
Cc
Dd
Ee
Ff
Gg
Hh
Ii
Jj
Kk
Ll
Mm
Nn
Oo
Pp
Qq
Rr
Ss
Tt
Uu
Vv
Ww
Xx
Yy
Zz

Zip

Zip is a friendly space alien from planet Zee. He loves to learn. Zip uses his hands to speak to his friends. He can't wait to teach the people of planet Earth all about sign language. Zip is the captain of his spaceship.

Pella

Pella is Zip's best friend. She also comes from planet Zee. Pella is very brave. Although she is a little younger than Zip and Statz, she isn't afraid of anything and is always the first of the three friends to try new things.

Statz

Statz is in charge of computers on the spaceship. He loves gadgets. Statz uses his Zablet to help him and his friends out of sticky situations. He is excited to learn about planet Earth and all the people who live here.

Goober

Goober is an unexpected guest on the friends' adventures. A greedy and naughty space stowaway, Goober has the ability to change his colour and shape so is always jumping out and surprising Zip, Pella and Statz.

Zip's top tips

Zip and friends are here to help you talk in a fun new way - spell with your fingers and talk with your hands. Follow these top tips to get the most from their adventures:

- **Share the book together and enjoy the story**
- **Play with the signs**
- **Use Zip's alphabet to make your own words**
- **Visit Space School, enjoy the activities and have fun**
- **Watch out for Goober...**

SignSpell

Zip and the Outdoor Adventure

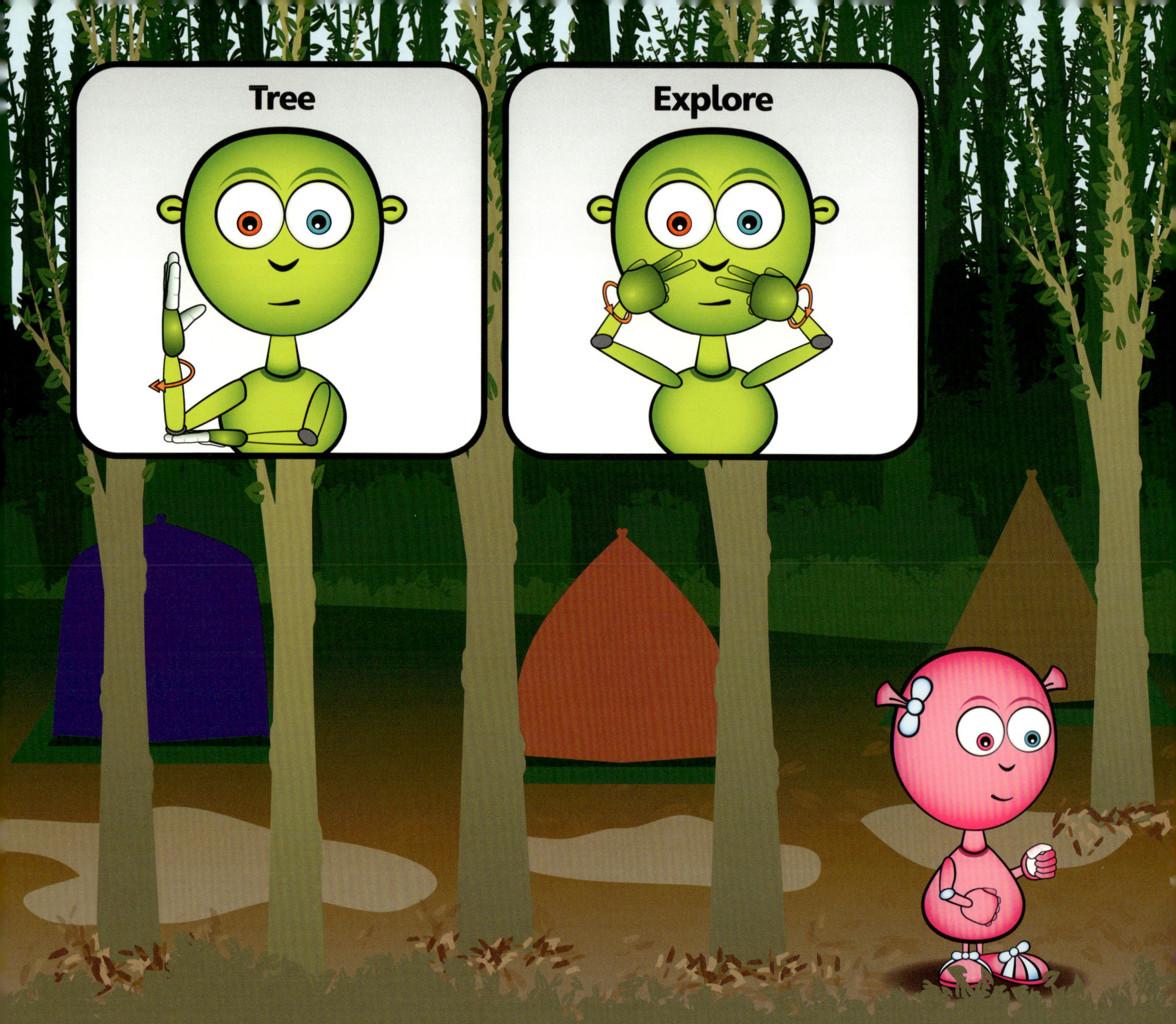

The spaceship has landed in a forest. Walking down the steps of the spaceship, Zip, Pella and Statz can see something between the trees.

"What are those funny shaped things over there?" asks Pella.

Statz uses his Zablet to find out what they are. “They are tents,” he tells his friends.
“Humans sometimes sleep in them when they want to explore the outdoors.”

The friends think it would be lots of fun to sleep in the great outdoors. They will need a tent big enough for three and soon find one they can use.

Zip and Pella lay all the pieces out on the ground.

Statz is studying the instructions on his Zablet, but the others don't want to wait.

Tent
10:06
Camping
FRONT
TOP
SIDE
< Page 01 of 3267 >

Zip and Pella each grab a pole and in no time at all, the tent is up. They stand back to admire their work.

"It doesn't look like any of the other tents," says Zip.

"Let's start again," says Statz, "and this time let's follow the instructions."

River
Bridge

The tent goes up quickly with the help of the instructions.
"That's it," says Zip. "Time to explore."
"It looks brilliant," says Pella.

"There's a nice long walk starting here," says Statz.
"We have to go down this path and find a way to cross the river."

"I can see where we need to go," says Zip, pointing at a bridge in the distance.

The friends set off on their walk.

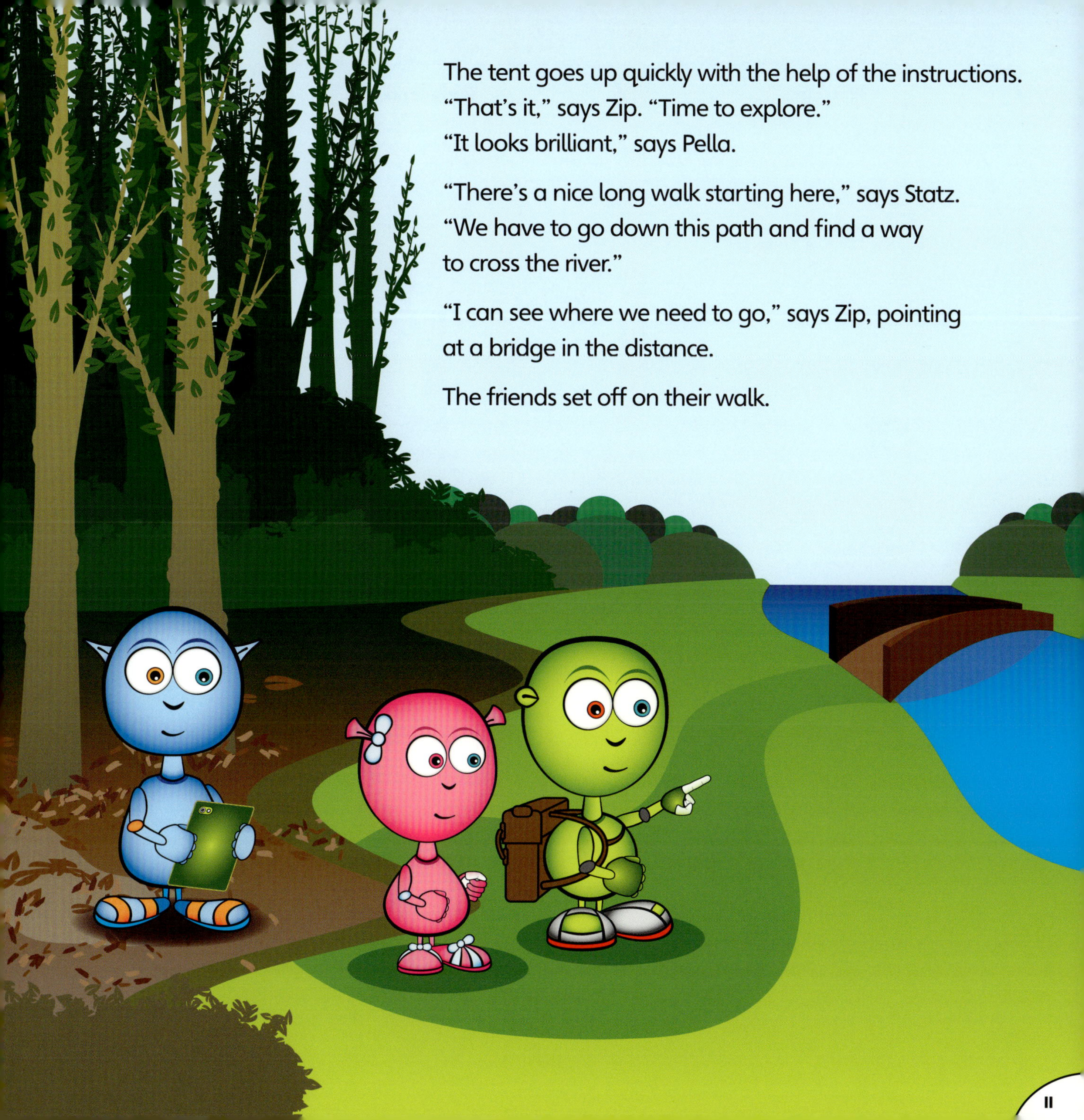

On the other side of the river, the friends stumble upon a sign. "Adventure Hike," says Statz. "That sounds like fun."

"Let's follow the trail," says Zip.

The friends set off and the path leads them deep into the forest. They notice something blocking the path.

ADVENTURE
HIKE

The path is blocked by a wall made of tree trunks. It is far too high for the friends to see over.

Zip jumps as high as he can, but he can't quite reach the top. Pella and Statz help him up.

Zip climbs over the top and hangs on to the wall, too scared to let go. "I can't reach the ground," he says. "I'm stuck. Help me!"

Pella and Statz help each other to the top of the wall. "Your feet are nearly touching a step," says Pella. "Just let go."

Space School

Take a look at the photograph on Statz's Zablet. Can you see some of the words you have learnt to sign from the story? See if you can spell each one using Zip's alphabet.

The friends are soon on their way again. A little further along, the path is blocked again. They see a sign low down on the ground that points to a hole.

"It's a tunnel," says Pella looking into the hole. "It's very dark down there."

"No problem," says Zip, "I will light the way." He leads the others down into the darkness.

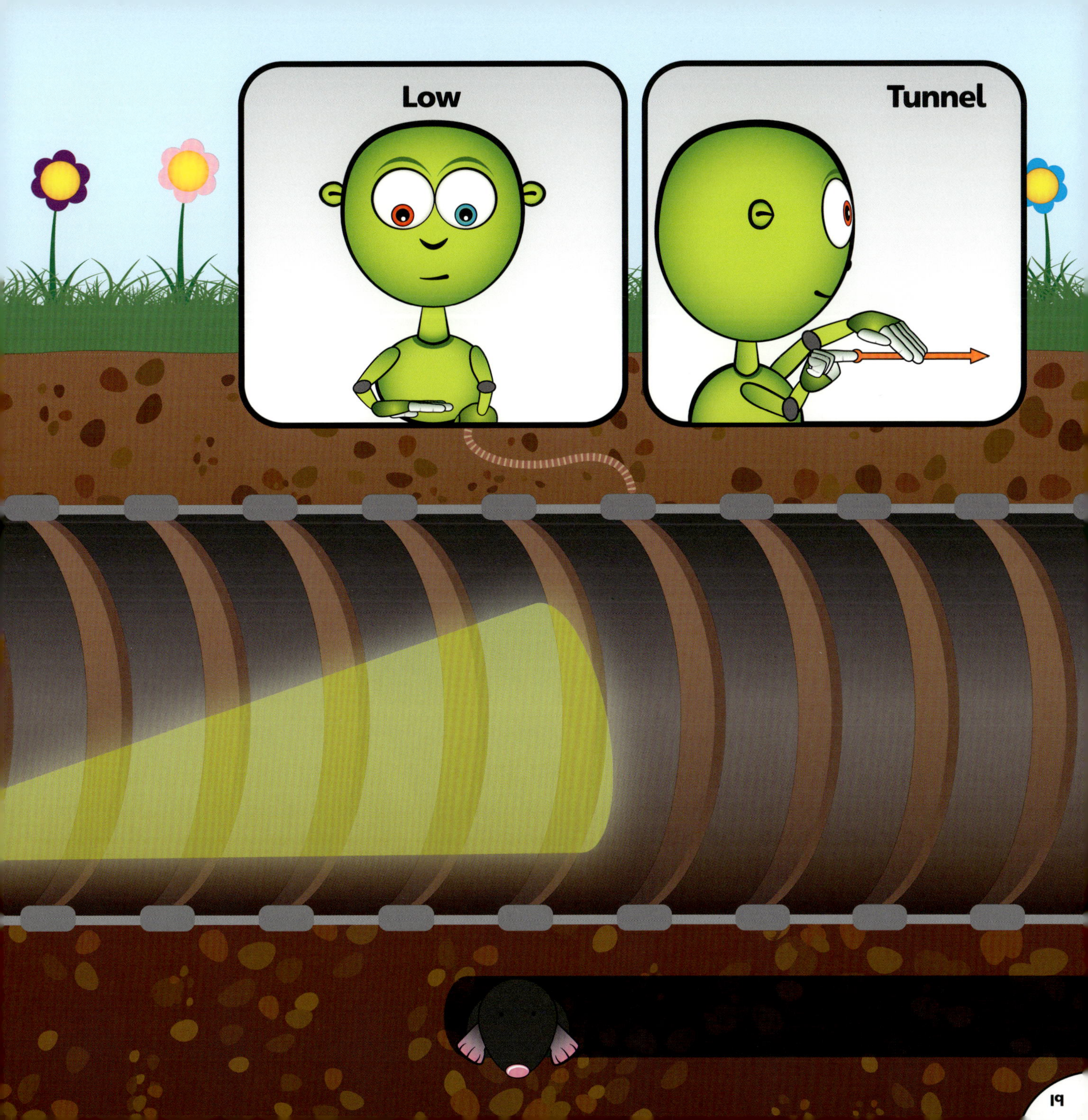
Low
Tunnel

The tunnel leads the friends to a wide open space. They see humans whizzing through the sky above on wires.

“That looks fun,” says Zip. They all climb the rope net to reach the platform high above the ground.

Climb
x4

The friends put on harnesses and are clipped to a wire.

"All together," says Zip. "One. Two. Three. Go!"

They take a step forward and jump off the platform, sliding down the wire at high speed.

After their big outdoor adventure, it is dark when the friends arrive back at camp.
The friends are very tired and want to get straight into their sleeping bags.

Space School

Take a look at the pictures below.
Can you remember how to sign them?

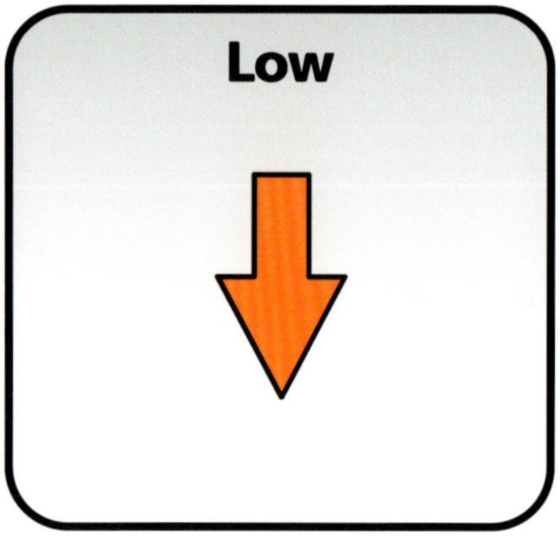

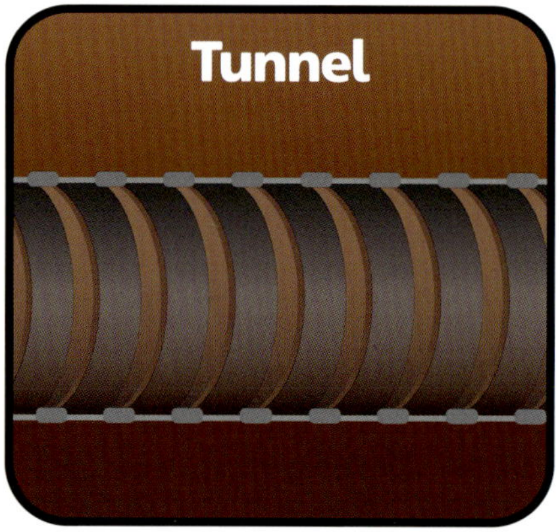

In the light of their torches the friends can see something has happened to their tent.

“It’s collapsed,” says Zip. “There is something moving under there.”

Statz slowly lifts the edge of the tent to peer underneath.

GOOBER!

Zip's Signs

Tree
Explore
Tent
River
Bridge
Wall
High
Low
Tunnel
Climb
x4

Fun things to do

Now that you have read all about Zip and the Outdoor Adventure,
here are some fun things for you to do:

- **Create your own tent - draw, describe or make**
- **What would you need to take with you on an outdoor adventure?**
- **How would you feel if you were flying through the air on a wire?**
- **During an adventure hike on planet Zee, what could block Zip's path?**
- **What would you do if your tent had collapsed?**
- **Teach a friend the signs for high and low**

First published 2013 by Signature

SignSpell® stories created by Signature
Designed and illustrated by Igloo Imaging Ltd.